Patchwork Puzzle Balls

Jinny Beyer

Breckling Press

Library of Congress Cataloging in Publication Data

Beyer, Jinny.

   Patchwork puzzle balls : fast, fun projects from simple shapes / Jinny Beyer.

      p. cm.

   Includes bibliographical references.

   ISBN 0-9721218-5-4

1. Decorative balls. 2. Patchwork—Patterns. 3. Textile fabrics. I. Title.

   TT896.8.B48 2005

   746.46′043—dc22

                           2004025176

This book was set in TheSans by Bartko Design
Editorial and production direction by Anne Knudsen
Art direction, cover and interior design by Kim Bartko
Photography by Sharon Hoogstraten
Technical drawings by Jinny Beyer and Kandy Petersen

Published by Breckling Press
283 Michigan St.
Elmhurst, IL 60126 USA

Printed and bound in China.

International Standard Book Number: 0-9721-2185-4

BALLS HAVE BEEN A FAVORITE SHAPE since the beginning of civilization, ever since bowling balls were found in Egypt way back in 5200 BC. In Medieval times, an inflated pig bladder made a perfect kick-around for an early game of hacky sack. And, of course, juggling has been a popular entertainment for more than 4000 years. Now it is time for patchwork designs in fabric to make their contribution.

Special thanks to Carole Nicholas who helped inspire Patchwork Puzzle Balls and who made many of the samples photographed. Thanks also to my friends who provided balls for photography, including Bonnie Campbell, Sandi Hettler, Barbara Hollinger, Julie Riggles, Gaye Ropp, Ricki Selva, Terri Willet, and my grandniece Savannah Sales. How can patchwork be any more fun?

Contents

A Word from Jinny

HERE I AM, the one who almost failed high-school geometry, getting involved with crystallography, mathematical models, and *polyhedra*. But don't let those big words scare you. For centuries, three-dimensional models made from simple shapes have been of as much interest to artists as they have to mathematicians. Simply speaking, when flat shapes are made into models, it is typically done from cardboard, plastic, metal or other hard materials, resulting in such forms as building blocks or many-sided dice. When those same shapes are made from soft fabric and are tightly stuffed with cotton, they magically transform into perfectly round balls.

It was my love of the geometry behind patchwork designs that first made me experiment with three-dimensional images in quilts. I wondered how the shapes in a flat quilt could so trick the eye that the viewer had the illusion of a third dimension. If you have ever looked at a traditional *Tumbling Blocks* quilt, you will know exactly what I mean. This question led me to a study of *polyhedra*, defined in the *Oxford English Reference Dictionary* as "solid figures with many faces." If you are familiar with my earlier book, *Designing Tessellations*, you will see this was a subject I had studied very seriously. But it was my friend Carole Nicholas who suggested a more light-hearted take on the topic. The same *polyhedra* that fascinate mathematicians can suggest fun and easy patchwork projects for people who love to sew.

Here is how the idea for *Patchwork Puzzle Balls* came about. Carole and I were discussing ideas for small projects to teach in my shop. Showing me her grandson's colorful soccer ball, Carole suggested we try to replicate it in fabric. We analyzed the ball, figuring out exactly how the basic patchwork shapes in its design were used and how the colors were balanced. I went back to my math books and discovered that the soccer ball design is based on a mathematical model that is much less difficult to understand than it sounds—a *truncated icosahedron*. Now, there was no stopping us. Not only did we re-create the soccer ball pattern in fabric, but we found many, many more *polyhedra* that magically transform into perfect spheres. When we introduced the designs to our students, the response was overwhelming. Everyone excitedly set out to make balls of their own—and they didn't stop at just one, but made many soft, beautiful balls in wonderful colors and fabrics. I have had such fun in creating my own variations—from balls made entirely from a simple shape, such as a triangle or a pentagon, to more intricate "tessellating" balls in the tradition of M.C. Escher. Best of all, the balls can be completed so quickly that my students call them projects for "instant gratification."

After the balls are made, people young and old seem to get a special joy out of holding them. I don't know if it is because of the patchwork designs, the fabrics, or the soft feel of the stuffed shape. Whether you use them for pillows or display, play catch with them, learn to juggle, or make them as baby gifts, the balls will give you quiet moments as you stitch and endless hours of fun once they are complete. So go to your fabric stash and let's all have a ball!

Jenny Dreyer

Let's Get Started!

IT IS CERTAINLY A PUZZLE to look at a series of flat shapes, such as triangles, pentagons, or octagons, and try to figure out how to transform them into perfectly round shapes. But we will leave that dilemma to mathematicians and just have fun with their results.

The first nine patterns in *Patchwork Puzzle Balls* are made from one or more of five basic shapes—triangle, square, pentagon, hexagon, or octagon. These shapes all share one common element—the length of every side is identical. This means that the shapes can be fitted together in multiple arrangements to form a

Embellished ball opposite is Job's Trouble *by Bonnie Campbell.*

variety of patterns. The first five templates on pages 85–86 are the only ones you will need to make any of these first nine balls.

Fabric Selection

The projects in *Patchwork Puzzle Balls* are perfect for using up odd scraps of favorite fabrics that are left over from larger sewing projects. If you are purchasing fabric, you will need at most a quarter yard of each color, usually quite a bit less. Make sure you pay attention to color values as you choose your fabrics—if there is not enough contrast among values, the individual patchwork shapes that make up the ball will not be distinct. Each pattern provides help with choosing fabrics that achieve the right contrast.

PATCHWORK PUZZLE TEMPLATES

Paper templates for all the basic shapes are provided on pages 85–86. Since you will be using the same basic shapes again and again as you experiment with different designs, *Patchwork Puzzle Balls* is accompanied by a set of durable plastic templates (sold separately). To increase accuracy, a hole is pre-punched at each angle, so that it is easy to match up angles or line up the different shapes. Simply use a sharp pencil to mark through the dot at the exact spot where you will start and stop sewing. *Puzzle Ball Templates* are available from Breckling Press.

The last four patterns in *Patchwork Puzzle Balls* require shapes other than a basic triangle, square, pentagon, hexagon, or octagon. Templates for these patterns are provided on pages 86–87. These four designs are a little more challenging in construction and will help you improve your sewing skills. The first two, *Tumbling Blocks* and *Desert Rose* are similar to the first nine balls and are relatively easy to construct. The last two,

Fabric Chart

For each ball, colors are arranged so than no two patches of the same color are allowed to touch each other. The best way to keep track of the colors and avoid mistakes is to make a fabric chart. For each project, photocopy the fabric chart on page 88. Cut small swatches of each your selected fabrics and glue or staple them onto the squares in the chart.

Making Templates

As noted on page 6, a companion set of templates is available to help speed up preparation time. If you prefer, it is easy to make your own templates.

Whirligig and *ZZZs* are tessellating designs in the style of M.C. Escher. The interlocking motifs in these balls require more setting in of seams than the other patterns, and it is a visual challenge to get all the pieces in the right places. The key is to pay close attention to the color placement illustrated in the diagrams. Because of the numerous angles to be set in, these last two patterns are best pieced by hand.

Making fabric puzzle balls is easy and fun. At times, it may seem that the pieces of the puzzle are not fitting together as they should. But if you keep going and make sure that you are following the diagrams carefully, all will come out well in the end. Before you begin,the remainder of this chapter will give you a few general guidelines that apply to all of the designs in the book. As you begin each new project, take a few minutes to refresh your memory on specific techniques described here.

1. Place a sheet of semi-transparent template plastic (available at most craft and quilt stores) over the desired template pattern on pages 85–87. Trace all markings, including the sewing line and the dots at each angle. (The dotted line indicates the sewing line; the solid line—an exact ¼″ outside the sewing line—indicates the cutting line.)

2. With sharp scissors, cut out the shape. Using a sixteenth inch hole punch, make a small hole in the template at each marked angle. (The holes indicate the exact spots where you will start and stop sewing.)

SUPPLIES CHECKLIST

In addition to basic sewing supplies like needles, threads, thimbles, and a sewing machine (optional), keep the following nearby.

- ☑ Semi-transparent template plastic
- ☑ Sharp scissors for cutting template plastic
- ☑ Sixteenth inch hole punch (optional)
- ☑ Sharp fabric scissors
- ☑ Rotary cutter and cutting mat (optional)
- ☑ Tailor's chalk or other fabric marker
- ☑ Chopstick or dollmaker's awl

Cutting Out Shapes

Each pattern indicates the number of fabric pieces to cut for each shape. For most patterns, you can cut two at a time by folding the fabric before cutting. The exceptions are *Whirligig* and *ZZZs*. (The reason is that these shapes are directional and pieces must all be cut right side up.) For any of the designs, it is possible to cut up to four shapes at a time by stacking layers of fabric right side up and using sharp scissors or a rotary cutter. You may want to put a couple of pins in the layers to keep them from slipping as you cut.

Mark clearly around each template before cutting. My preferred marker is tailors' chalk. The Clover Company makes a good brand, shaped in a triangle and sharp on all three sides. When the edges become dull, it's easy to sharpen them again with an emery board, a knife, or an old pair of scissors. Cut just within the chalk line to get fabric pieces that are exactly the same size as the templates.

Sewing

Since the patches are small and most patterns require some *setting in* of pieces, I find it easiest to stitch the balls by hand. They make perfect carry-along projects and you will be amazed at how quickly you complete your first ball. If you prefer to stitch by machine, the first couple of steps in each pattern—while everything is still flat—are easy to do. Once the dimensional shape of the ball starts evolving, it is easier to complete by hand. The balls will be stuffed very tightly, so—whether sewing by hand or machine—it is important that stitches are secure. For machine sewing, set the stitch length so that stitches are very close together and backstitch at the beginning and end of each seam; for hand-sewing, make the stitches as small as possible and backstitch every few stitches and at the beginning and end of each seam.

Setting In

The pattern *Thousand Pyramids* on page 22 is the only design in *Patchwork Puzzle Balls* that can be sewn entirely with straight seams. All other patterns require that some patches are set into a Y-seam created by two other patches. When setting in pieces like this, the key is to stop all stitching at precisely the spot where the seam allowances on the pieces cross. This allows for an opening so the pieces to be set in can be sewn smoothly and without puckers.

The best way of knowing exactly where to start and stop stitching, is to mark small dots on each fabric patch at the points where seam allowances cross. Those points are already marked for you on the templates on pages 85 to 87. As directed above, simply transfer those markings from your templates onto your fabrics when you are

THREAD COLOR

Because the balls are stuffed very tightly, the stitches are apt to show. This means that the thread you select for stitching is very important. It may even be necessary to use more than one thread color, depending on the contrast between patches you are sewing together. Never use white or very light-colored thread unless your patches are white or very light. When sewing two patches together, match the thread to the darker colored patch, not the lighter one. I keep spools of thread in black, navy, burgundy, brown, and light gray (for very light patches) always at hand. I find one or other of these basic thread colors will usually work well.

PATCHWORK PUZZLE BALLS IN FIVE EASY STEPS

All of the balls are contructed in the same way. The photographs here show how one of the designs, *Snowballs* on page 26, comes together. Use the same simple steps for every pattern.

1. Cut out the required pieces for each half-ball. To make the first half of *Snowballs* you will need three squares and four hexagons.

2. Lay out the pieces as shown in the pattern illustrations. Place a marker pin in the patch indicated in the pattern. Sew the patches together, beginning and ending exactly at the spot where the seam allowances intersect. The work is still flat at this point.

10

3. Sew the remaining seams to create the dimensional half-ball shape.

4. Make the second half-ball in the same way. Position the two half-balls so that the patches you pinned in Step 2 lie next to each other. Right sides facing, sew these patches together first. Continue sewing until only one seam remains unstitched. Turn right side out.

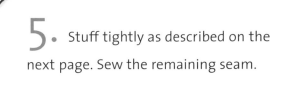

5. Stuff tightly as described on the next page. Sew the remaining seam.

11

cutting. Note, too, that the plastic templates that accompany this book already have holes pre-punched at the angle, so that you can easily mark the point at which seam allowances cross (see page 6).

To set in a piece, follow these steps.

1. Use the template to mark each seam intersection.
2. Rights sides together, pin the patch to be set in to one of the adjacent pieces, matching the marks at the seam intersections.
3. Sew from the raw edge toward the set-in corner. As you approach the corner, pull the seam allowances to the left and stitch just to the corner dot. To ensure a tight intersection, take a back stitch, with the needle coming up right at the dot. Do not cut the thread.
4. Pivot the patch being set in and pin it to the next piece. Continue sewing the seam from the corner out, stopping at the mark along this sewing line.

Pressing

The balls will be stuffed so tight, that it really isn't necessary to press the pieces, but when the sections for each half-ball are still flat, I usually press them gently. Lay them right side up on a thick, fluffy towel, letting the seam allowances fall in whatever direction they want to go. Press lightly.

Stuffing and Finishing

How the balls are stuffed is one of the most important parts in the whole process. You have to remember that if the designs were made up in a stiff material, such as cardboard or plastic, the end result would be a many-sided shape on which each face is perfectly flat. When balls made from fabric from these same flat shapes are stuffed, they become round because of the flexibility of the fabric. It is important, though, to stuff them *very tightly* to keep that round shape. I prefer a 100 percent cotton stuffing material (not batting, because it will be lumpy). I like Quilters Dream Cotton. Polyester stuffing is not dense enough to hold a firm shape. A one pound bag of 100 percent cotton stuffing will stuff one large ball (approximately 7" diameter) and one small ball (approximately 4" diameter). The same bag will stuff two medium-sized balls. This is the process I use for stuffing.

1. Complete all sewing of the ball except for a single seam. Make sure the seams at the opening are double stitched so they do not come apart. Turn the ball right side out.

2. Take some cotton stuffing and separate it with your fingers into small wisps. (If you insert it in clumps straight from bag, the ball will be lumpy.)

3. Taking care not to put stress on the seams close to the opening, begin inserting stuffing.

4. Once the ball is reasonably well stuffed, use a utensil such as a wooden or plastic chopstick, a cooking-spoon handle, or a doll-maker's awl to compact the stuffing as much as possible. (When you think you have ball as full as it can be, you probably need half as much stuffing again.) Work the chopstick to the side of the ball opposite the opening until you can feel the end of it through the fabric. Work the stuffing around that patch until it is very tight. Use your fingers to feel for soft spots on any part of the ball. When you find soft spots, work the chopstick to that section and keep pushing stuffing against it. You will find that the channel where the chopstick worked its way to the opposite side now needs more stuffing. Take little bits of the cotton and push them into the channel with the chopstick.

LET'S ALL HAVE A BALL

Once you begin making Patchwork Puzzle Balls, you'll find it's hard to stop! Here are some idea-starters for balls to make as gifts. Once you've made one or two balls, the designs become so easy, it's child's play!

EMBELLISHMENT
Buttons, beads, ribbons and fancy threads—the sky's the limit!

GEOMETRY LESSON
Play with shapes and sew up a ball for an unforgettable geometry class

SOCCER BALL FOR COACH
Photo-transfer the smiling faces of players onto the fabric for an end-of-season gift

MATH MAGIC
Have children autograph the tessellating ZZZs ball as a playful teacher gift

HOLIDAY CHEER
Whip up multi-sized balls in seasonal fabrics

5. When the ball is as full as can be, put two thumbs into the opening and push the stuffing to the edges of the ball all around the opening. You will find that there is still room for more stuffing. Gently push in more stuffing around the opening.

6. Let the ball sit overnight. The cotton will compact and by morning the ball will be ready for yet more stuffing.

7. When you are finally ready to stitch the final seam, close the opening with a small whip stitch. When all but about half an inch remains, secure with a knot. Do not cut the thread. Gently push more stuffing into the hole and around the stitched-up final seam.

8. Sew another few stitches and gently work more wisps into the hole before finally closing the opening completely.

9. Place the completed ball in the dryer along with a slightly damp towel and spin for about five minutes. This will plump up the stuffing and make the ball nice and round. If at a later time, the ball appears out of shape, repeat this process.

Perfect Spheres from Basic Shapes

ALL THE BALLS IN THIS SECTION are made from one or more of five basic shapes—triangle, square, pentagon, hexagon, and octagon. If you would like to make your ball larger or smaller than the patterns here provide for, it's easy to redraft the shapes following the directions on pages 75–84. Quick, easy, and fun, these designs invite you to play with fabric in ways you never have before!

Bat Wings

Mathematical model: *Dodecahedron*   **Diameter:** 4″   **Template 3**

*About the size of a softball, **Bat Wings** is perfect for playing catch—or make three and learn to juggle! The design is similar to a traditional patchwork pattern also known as **Bat Wings**; it is a simple five-sided shape with identical angles. The puzzle here is simple—twelve pentagons in a range of colors are positioned so that same-color pieces never touch. **Bat Wings** has the fewest pieces of all the designs in **Patchwork Puzzle Balls**. It makes a perfect beginner project and can be completed in just a couple of hours.*

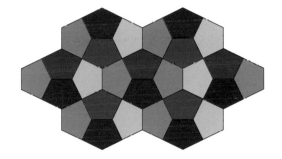

Traditional pattern

Color Clues

Six different fabrics are needed for this project. Look at the photo and you will see that each color pentagon touches every other color—make sure there is enough contrast between your selected fabrics so that each pentagon is easily distinguishable from the others. Note that same-color pentagons always lie on directly opposite sides of the ball. Carefully adhere to the colors indicated on the diagrams and you will achieve the same effect. Copy the fabric chart on page 88 and staple or glue your fabric swatches to it.

Cutting Clues

Cut **12 pentagons** (two from each of six fabrics) using **Template 3** on page 85. Template includes ¼″ seam allowance. Speed up cutting time by using the pre-made template set that accompanies this book.

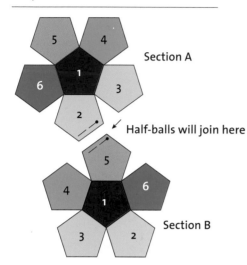

Section A

Half-balls will join here

Section B

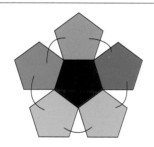

Solving the Puzzle

The easiest way to construct this ball is to sew two halves, then stitch them together. Follow these steps:

1. Lay out the fabric pentagons as shown, with Fabric 1 at the center and the remaining fabrics surrounding it. Note that in Section A, Fabrics 2 to 6 are positioned counter-clockwise around Fabric 1, while in Section B placement is clockwise. Maintain this order of placement to ensure that same-color fabrics do not touch each other. Mark or place pins in Fabric 2, Section A, and in Fabric 5, Section B. Once both halves of ball are complete, this is where you will begin sewing them together.

2. Keeping a continuous thread for each section, pick up each pentagon in order of placement and sew it to the center piece. Press lightly.

3. Sew the sides of the pentagons together as shown, creating a half-ball shape.

4. Right sides together, orient the halves so that pre-marked Fabrics 2 and 5 are aligned. Pin the seam. Carefully sew the halves together, pivoting the fabric at each side of the pentagons. Sew until only one seam remains unstitched.

5. Carefully turn the ball right side out. Stuff and finish (see pages 12–15).

SAVANNAH'S *BAT WINGS*

Every summer my grandniece Savannah visits and we always do a sewing project together. When she was younger, I would cut out large patches for her to arrange as she pleased, then I would double-thread a needle for her (so she would not lose the thread), make a knot, and watch her sew the pieces together. Last summer, Savannah's cousin Doone came with her. When both of these nine-year-olds saw the balls I had been making for *Patchwork Puzzle Balls*, they immediately decided to make one, too. Since Savannah and Doone were now old enough to work by themselves, I showed them how to thread the needle, tie the knot, and sew with a single thread. They learned how to mark a ¼" seam allowance, made a perfect running stitch, and quickly mastered the trick of pivoting patches that were to be set in.

Bat Wings was the ideal choice as a first pattern for the girls. The design has only twelve pieces and it comes together fairly quickly. I gave Savannah and Doone a big box of fabric squares, telling them to find six fabrics each that looked good together but were distinct enough so that they stood out from one another. Next, the girls cut their own pieces, arranged them in the proper order, and began to sew. In less than three hours the balls were complete. Savannah and Doone were so proud of their accomplishments, especially since they had made the balls entirely on their own. Savannah decided to take her ball home, but asked, "If I make another one, do you think you could send it to your publisher and include it in your book?" Of course, I told

her I would. Savannah immediately selected fabrics and made the ball you see here.

When I was growing up my grandmother and my mother taught me to sew. Girls were required to take home economics, and we sewed there as well. Today, perhaps because so many women work, there seems to be less time to sit with our children and teach them to sew. Even if it's only for a half an hour each week, it is important to take time to pass basic sewing skills down to our children—and what better way to start than to make a ball! A project like this is perfect for young children, since it teaches basic techniques and can be quickly completed. The next time you have the opportunity for quiet time with a young child, pull out your fabric stash. Sit down together, select fabrics, and sew!

Thousand Pyramids

Mathematical model: *Icosahedron*   **Diameter:** 2³/₄″   **Template 1**

*The smallest of all of the balls, **Thousand Pyramids** is made from 20 triangles. It makes a perfect juggling ball or—by adding a bell inside—you can easily turn it into a fun toy for your pet to bat around. It's also a nice, soft toy for baby—try hanging three or four colorful balls from a mobile above the crib. To make a larger ball in the same design, simply draft an equilateral triangle in the size of your choice (see page 76). These balls, made by Carole Nicholas, are the easiest of all the patterns in this book to sew by machine.*

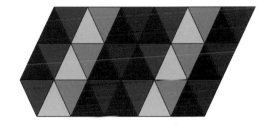

Traditional pattern

Color Clues

Five different fabrics are required for *Thousand Pyramids*. Notice from the photo that a triangle of each color touches all other colors. It is important to select fabrics carefully so that all triangles are easily distinguishable. Also note that the placement of the colors is evenly distributed around the ball, so be sure to follow the diagrams carefully when sewing pieces together. Copy the fabric chart on page 88 and staple or glue your fabric swatches to it.

Cutting Clues

Cut **20 triangles** (four from each of five fabrics) using **Template 1** on page 85. Template includes ¼″ seam allowance. Speed up cutting time by using the pre-made template set that accompanies this book.

Solving the Puzzle

Thousand Pyramids is constructed in two halves. Once the two halves are complete, you may think you made a mistake, because there will be distinct "points" and you may wonder how on earth the piece will turn into a perfect sphere. But don't worry—once the fabric is well stuffed, you will have a perfectly round ball. Follow these steps:

1. Lay out the triangle fabrics as shown for each ball half (Section A and Section B). Carefully follow the color placement in the diagram. Mark or place pins as shown in the right-most Fabric 4 in Section A and in the left-most Fabric 1 in Section B. Once both halves of the ball are complete, this is where you will begin sewing them together.

Step 1

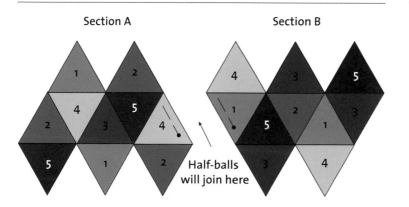

Half-balls will join here

Step 2

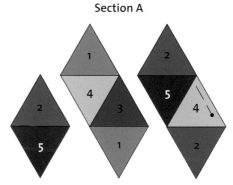

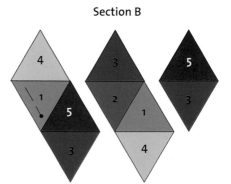

2. For each section, sew the shapes together in two rows of four triangles and one row of two triangles as shown. Use a continuous thread for four-triangle rows. Use straight seams to join the rows. Press lightly.

3. Sew the sides of the triangles together at the top and bottom of each section as shown, creating a half-ball shape.

4. Right sides together, orient the halves so that pre-marked Fabrics 4 and 1 are aligned. Pin the seam. Sew the halves together until only one seam remains unstitched.

5. Carefully turn the ball right side out. Stuff and finish (see pages 12–15).

Step 3

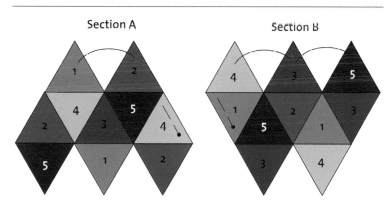

Section A   Section B

Snowballs

Mathematical model: *Truncated octahedron*   **Diameter:** 4³/₄"
Templates 2 and 4

The traditional quilt pattern, **Snowballs** *is made up of an octagon and a square. Here, in order to get the design to form a ball, the octagon changes to a hexagon. The ball is constructed from eight hexagons and six squares. With a total of only 14 pieces,* **Snowballs** *takes very little time to make. The photographs on page 10–11 show this design coming together.*

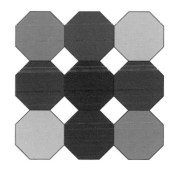

Traditional pattern

Color Clues

Five different fabrics are required to complete the ball. As you can see in the photograph of Carole Nicholas' *Snowballs*, the design stands out best when there is a sharp contrast between squares and hexagons. I recommend making the squares either very dark or very light, with the four hexagon fabrics of a medium value. Note that the design has same-color hexagons on opposite sides. Since any one hexagon touches each of the other three, make sure there is enough contrast between the fabrics so the hexagons will be distinguishable. Reserve Fabric 1 for the squares only. Copy the fabric chart on page 88 and staple or glue the swatches to it.

Cutting Clues

Cut **6 squares** from Fabric 1 using **Template 2** on page 85.
Cut **8 hexagons** (two from each of remaining fabrics) from **Template 4**. Templates include ¼" seam allowance. Speed up

cutting time by using the pre-made template set that accompanies this book.

Solving the Puzzle

To make the ball, first sew two halves then stitch them together. Follow theses steps:

1. Lay out the shapes for Section A and Section B as shown, making sure the numbers on your fabric chart correspond with the numbers on the diagram. Mark or place pins in Fabric 5, Section A and in Fabric 2, Section B. Once both halves of the ball are complete, this is where you will begin sewing them together.

Step 1

Section A

2   1   4   1   5   1

3

3

2   1   4   1   5

Half-balls will join here   Section B

Step 2

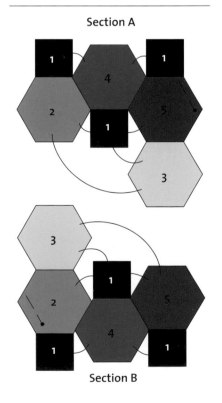

Section A

Section B

2. Follow the diagram to sew the pieces together. Press lightly.
3. Sew the sides of the shapes together as shown, creating a half-ball shape.
4. Right sides together, orient the two halves so that pre-marked Fabrics 5 and 2 are aligned. Pin the seam. Sew the halves together, pivoting the fabric as needed. Sew until only one seam remains unstitched.
5. Carefully turn the ball right side out. Stuff and finish (see pages 12–15).

ADD SOUND EFFECTS!

Have some fun and hide a noise-maker inside your ball. You might choose a bell, for instance, for a cat toy—it will give kitty hours of fun. Craft stores sell all kinds of easy-to-hide objects that make a noise when you squeeze them. JINNY BEYER STUDIO offers a range of noisemakers, even ones on which you can record your own message. What a great way to pass along your best wishes or a special message when you make a ball as a gift! Simply stuff the ball part way, insert the noisemaker, then finish stuffing. If your ball needs to be squeezed to make the sound, choose a pattern for one of the smaller balls, ike *Thousand Pyramids, Bat Wings,* or *Snowballs.*

Aunt Etta's Diamond

Mathematical model: *Icosidodecahedron*　　**Diameter:** 4¾"
Templates 1 and 3

---

*If you would like to make two balls of different design but in the
identical size, **Snowballs** on page 26 is the perfect companion to **Aunt
Etta's Diamond**. The design resembles a traditional quilt pattern of the
same name, but in order to form the ball the hexagon in the original
pattern is changed to a pentagon. Any direction the ball is turned will
show a five-pointed star; the star centers are the same color, each
surrounded by darker triangle points. The ball is made from
12 pentagons and 20 triangles.*

Color Clues

Aunt Etta's Diamond can be made from as few as two different
fabrics. The balls photographed here each use seven. The version in
the foreground was made by Bunnie Jordan. Careful arrangement of
colors will result in same-colored stars falling on opposite sides of
the ball. Color contrast from one pentagon to the next is not as
critical for this design as it is for others in *Patchwork Puzzle Balls*. The
reason is that the pentagons never touch each other. It is important,
however, to achieve good contrast between the center pentagons
and the surrounding triangles. Copy the fabric chart on page 88 and
staple or glue your fabric swatches to it.

Cutting Clues

Cut **20 triangles** from Fabric 1 using **Template 1** on page 85. Cut
12 pentagons (two from each of six fabrics) using **Template 3**. For a

Traditional pattern

simpler, two-color version, cut **20 triangles** using **Template 1** and **12 pentagons** in contrasting fabric using **Template 3**. Templates include ¼″ seam allowance. Speed up cutting time by using the pre-made template set that accompanies this book.

Solving the Puzzle

To make the ball, first sew two halves, then stitch them together. Follow these steps:

1. Make two stars using Fabric 7 pentagons at the center, surrounded by five Fabric 1 triangles as shown.
2. Sew one triangle to each of the remaining pentagons.
3. Sort the pentagons by color number and sew one of each color clockwise around the first star (Section A). Sew the remaining five

Step 2

UNUSUAL FABRICS AND FANCY STITCHING

If you are a quilter, your fabric stash probably consists mostly of 100 percent cottons. Because puzzle balls are small projects and are unlikely to be washed, why not try working with different fabrics? A ball made in wool, like *Bat Wings* shown here, holds its shape nicely and is very soft to the touch. This version of *Bat Wings* is embellished with feather-stitching along each seam. Perle cotton was used for the embroidery. The feather-stitching was started once the ball halves were completed and partially sewn together, but before stuffing. From there, as seams were sewn, the feather stitching continued. With one seam left, the ball was stuffed and the seam closed. Then the feather-stitching was completed over the final seam.

pentagons counter-clockwise around the second star (Section B) as shown. Press lightly. Mark or place pins in Fabric 2 in Section A and in Fabric 5 in Section B. Once both halves of the ball are complete, this is where you will begin sewing them together.

4. Sew the sides of the pentagons and triangles together as shown, creating a half-ball shape.

5. Right sides together, orient the halves so that pre-marked Fabrics 2 and 5 are aligned. Pin the seam. Sew the halves together until only one seam remains unstitched.

6. Carefully turn the ball right side out. Stuff and finish (see pages 12–15).

Step 3

Section A

Half-balls will join here

Section B

Step 4

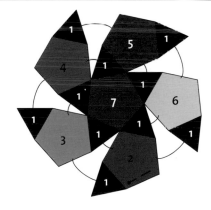

33

Soccer Ball

Mathematical model: *Truncated icosahedron*   **Diameter:** 7¼″
Templates 3 and 4

One of the larger balls in **Patchwork Puzzle Balls**, *this is a design that is very familiar to most of us. Every child has kicked around a soccer ball at some time or other, perhaps picking it up to wonder how the flat shapes it is made from create a round ball. With 12 pentagons and 20 hexagons, it is fun to make—and great for a game of indoor soccer when it is done.*

Color Clues

If you would like the design to look like a true soccer ball, make all the hexagons white and all the pentagons black. The design photographed, made by Carole Nicholas, uses seven different fabrics, with half the pentagons in an alternate color. The pattern below is just as effective with same-color pentagons. The key is that there must be contrast between each of the selected fabrics, as each one will touch all the others. Note that same-color fabrics are positioned directly opposite each other on the finished ball. For the Fabric 1 pentagons, choose a color that is either lighter or darker than all the others. Carefully adhere to the fabric numbers on the diagram so that two fabrics of the same color will not fall next to each other. Copy the fabric chart on page 88 and staple or glue your fabric swatches to it.

Cutting Clues

Cut **12 pentagons** from Fabric 1 using **Template 3** on page 85. Cut **20 hexagons** (four from each of remaining five fabrics) using

SIMPLE COLOR SCHEME, BEAUTIFUL BALL

While the *Soccer Ball* photographed on page 34 has as many as seven bright colors, you can make a lovely ball with a much simpler color scheme. See how carefully Terri Willett has arranged her black and white shapes to create a fun and playful soccer ball design. Wouldn't a cloth soccer ball with signatures or photos of everyone on the team make a perfect gift for the coach?

Template 4. Templates include ¼" seam allowance. Speed up cutting time by using the pre-made template set that accompanies this book.

Solving the Puzzle

The easiest way to construct this ball is to sew two halves and then stitch the two halves together. Follow these steps:

1. Lay out Section A and Section B exactly as shown for correct color placement. Mark or place pins in the right-most Fabric 3 hexagon in Section A and in the left-most Fabric 5 hexagon in Section B.

Step 1

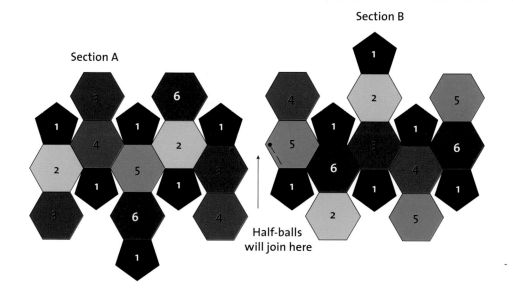

Once both halves of the ball are complete, this is where you will begin sewing them together.

2. Sew Sections A and B, joining the pieces exactly as shown. Press.

3. Sew the sides of the pentagons to the sides of the hexagons as shown, creating a half-ball shape.

4. Right sides together, orient the halves so that pre-marked Fabrics 3 and 5 are aligned. Pin the seam. Carefully sew the halves together, pivoting the fabric as needed. Sew until only one seam remains unstitched.

5. Carefully turn the ball right side out. Stuff and finish (see pages 12–15).

Step 3

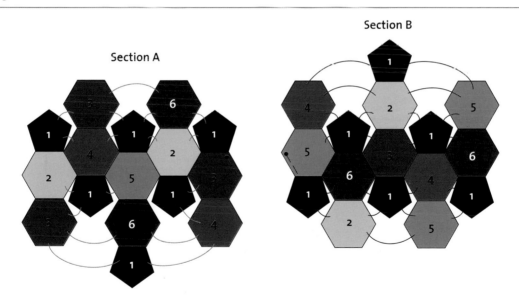

World Without End

Mathematical model: *Snub cube*   **Diameter:** 5″   **Templates 1 and 2**

*The name of the traditional pattern **World Without End** conjures up images of a pattern that goes on for ever. Transfer the design to a sphere and its interlocking stars appear to circle the world. There are a total of 38 pieces in the ball—six squares and 32 triangles. The stars are arranged so that matching pairs fall on opposite sides of the ball. Note in the photograph a variation of the ball using a decorative border-print fabric. (See also pages 48–49.)*

Color Clues

There are several options for coloring the four-pointed stars in this ball. For a calmer effect, make the star points and the center square from the same fabric, creating six solid-color stars that interlock. For a little more variation, make the center square from a darker fabric in the same family as the fabric used for the points, as shown in the ball on the far left, made by Sandi Hettler. Whatever you choose, the star points must be distinctly different from each other, as they all interlock and any one colored star touches all the others. There must be enough contrast in the three fabrics selected for the star points so they can be seen.

The small ball in the foreground of the photograph, made by Gaye Ropp, has matching pairs of three differently colored stars. The centers are lighter than the star points. There are eight extra triangles that are not part of the stars. These must contrast with the star points and must be either very dark or very light. In this sample, they are brown. All told, you may use as many seven different fabrics. Fabric 1 is the darkest or the lightest. Fabrics 2 and 3 are in the same

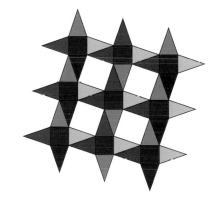

Traditional pattern

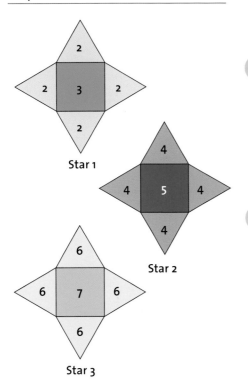

Star 1

Star 2

Star 3

color family but Fabric 3 is darker than Fabric 2. The same is true of Fabrics 4 and 5 and of Fabrics 6 and 7. Copy the fabric chart on page 88 and staple or glue your fabric swatches to it..

Cutting Clues

Cut **32 triangles** (8 from Fabric 1, then 8 each from Fabrics 2, 4 and 6) using **Template 1** on page 85. Cut **6 squares** (two each from Fabrics 3, 4, and 7) using **Template 2**. Templates include ¼" seam allowance. Speed up cutting time by using the pre-made template set that accompanies this book.

Solving the Puzzle

The easiest way to construct this ball is to sew two halves and then stitch the two halves together. Follow these steps:

1.   If you are working by hand, keep a continuous thread as you sew four Fabric 2 triangles around a Fabric 3 square as shown to complete Star 1. Make two. In the same way, make two more sets

ADD A THEME!

There are so many fun novelty fabrics available today that there are all kinds of way you can build a theme into your puzzle balls. For Valentine's Day, instead of a box of chocolates, give a ball made with candy-motif fabrics. Center holiday scenes in some of the pieces, or make a ball from patriotic red, white, and blue fabrics. For a child, put letters of the alphabet inside the shapes, or make a ball from pretty pastels—a perfect baby shower gift, made by Carole Nicholas.

of stars. Star 2 uses Fabric 4 triangles and Fabric 5 squares. Star 3 uses Fabric 6 triangles and Fabric 7 squares.

2. Following the diagram and taking care to orient the stars correctly, make Section A by sewing Stars 1, 2, and 3 together and adding four extra triangles from Fabric 1. Repeat for Section B. Press lightly.

3. Mark or place pins in the bottom-most Fabric 6 triangle in Section A and in the top-most Fabric 4 triangle in Section B. Once halves of the ball are complete, this is where you will begin sewing the halves together.

4. Sew the sides of the triangles together as shown, creating a half-ball shape.

5. Right sides together, orient the two halves so that pre-marked Fabrics 6 and 4 are aligned. Pin the seam. Carefully sew the halves together, pivoting the fabrics as needed, until only one seam remains unstitched.

6. Carefully turn the ball right side out. Stuff and finish (see pages 12–15).

Step 2

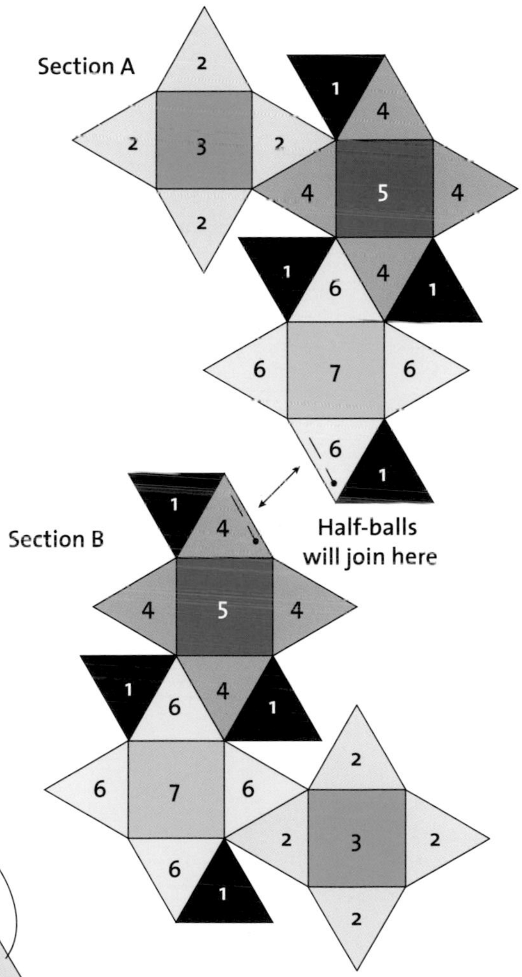

Section A

Section B

Half-balls will join here

Step 3

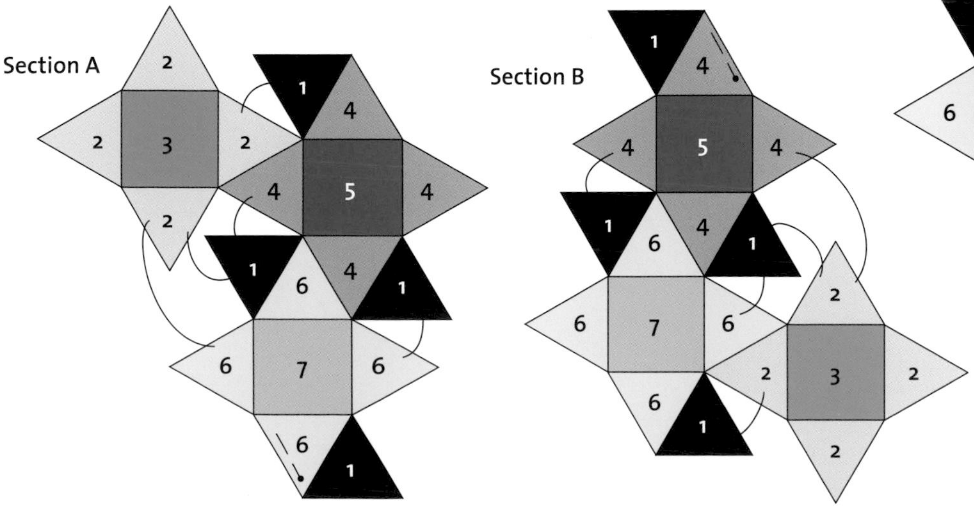

Section A

Section B

Spring Fling

Mathematical model: *Snub dodecahedron*   **Diameter:** 6⅝"

Templates 1 and 3

Spring Fling is very similar to **World Without End** on page 38. Both balls
have stars that overlap at the sides and both have extra triangles
positioned next to some of the star points. The difference is that **Spring
Fling** has a pentagon rather than a square at the center of the design.
There are also quite a few more pieces (92 instead of 38), so the ball is
larger. The stars are arranged so that matching pairs of stars fall on
opposite sides of the ball.

Color Clues

As with *World Without End*, there are several coloring options. For a
calmer effect, make the points of the star and the center pentagon
from the same fabric, creating six solid-colored interlocking stars.
Alternatively, keep the center pentagons the same and vary the star
points, as shown here. The center pentagon could be a darker fabric
of the same family as the points. Another interesting variation is to
use the same dark fabric for the center pentagons and the extra
triangles—the stars appear to float against a background. Whichever
variation you choose, be sure that the star points are distinct from
each other, since they will overlap, with any one star touching all
others. To make them visible, there must be enough contrast in the
six fabrics selected for the star points.

   The ball photographed here has two each of six differently colored
star points. While the fabric for the points is of medium value, every
selection is distinguishable from each of the others. There are

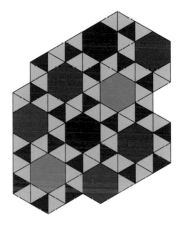

Traditional pattern

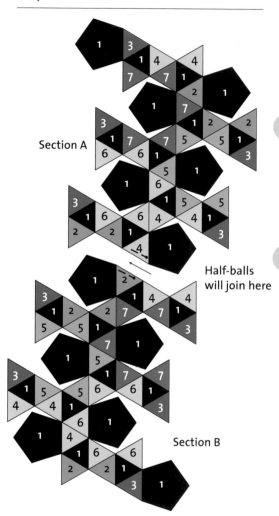

Section A

Half-balls
will join here

Section B

20 extra triangles that are not part of the stars. These must contrast with the star points and must be either very dark or very light. The pentagons at the center are made from the same fabric. In all, you will need seven different fabrics. Fabric 1 is the darkest or lightest and the remaining fabrics are for the star points. Copy the fabric chart on page 88 and staple or glue your fabric swatches to it.

Cutting Clues

Cut **80 triangles** (20 from Fabric 1, then 10 each from Fabrics 2 to 7) using **Template 1** on page 85. Cut **12 pentagons** from Fabric 1 using **Template 3**. Templates include ¼" seam allowance. Speed up cutting time by using the pre-made template set that accompanies this book.

Solving the Puzzle

The easiest way to construct this ball is to sew two halves and then stitch the two halves together. To ensure that same-color fabrics do not touch each other, look carefully at fabric placement in the first diagram. Follow these steps:

1. Lay out the fabric pentagons and triangles for Sections A and B as shown. Mark or place pins in the bottom-most Fabric 4 in Section A and in the top-most Fabric 2 in Section B. Once both halves of the ball are complete, this is where you will begin sewing them together.

2. Join the pentagons and triangles as shown in the previous diagram. If you are hand sewing, avoid knots by sewing with a continuous thread. Press lightly.

3. Sew the sides of the triangles to the sides of each pentagon as shown, creating a half-ball shape.

4. Right sides together, orient the two halves so that pre-marked Fabrics 4 and 2 are aligned. Pin the seam. Carefully sew the halves together, pivoting the fabrics as needed. Sew until only one seam remains unstitched.

5. Carefully turn the ball right side out. Stuff and finish (see pages 12–15).

Step 2

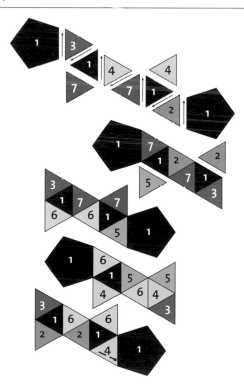

Step 3

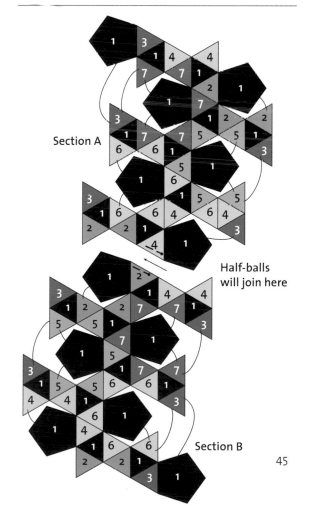

Section A

Half-balls will join here

Section B

45

Job's Trouble

Mathematical model: *Great rhombicuboctahedron*

Diameter: 7¼"   **Templates 2, 4, and 5**

*Very similar in design to **Snowballs** on page 24, Job's Trouble is made from three shapes instead of two. There are more pieces, too—26 instead of 14. Constructed from six octagons, eight hexagons and 12 squares, there are many design choices when planning colors for this ball. Look, for instance, at the design of the smaller ball. Here, the octagons are broken into triangles then cut from a decorative border-print fabric.*

Color Clues

Experiment with the many options for coloring this ball. A pretty three-fabric combination is to use one color for each of the squares, another for the hexagons, and a third for the octagons. If you would like to add more color, use three fabrics for the octagons, four for the hexagons, and one for the squares. In the ball photographed here, made by Gaye Ropp, all squares are in one fabric, while four different fabrics are used for the hexagons and six for the octagons. Even though none of the hexagons touch each other, this color combination balances color effectively around the ball. For accurate color placement, study the first diagram below before you begin. Copy the fabric chart on page 88 and staple or glue your fabric swatches to it.

Cutting Clues

Cut **6 octagons** from Fabric 1 using **Template 5** on page 86. Cut **12 squares** from Fabric 2 using **Template 2**. Cut **8 hexagons** (2 each

47

SPECIAL EFFECTS WITH DECORATIVE FABRICS

Specialty fabrics can do a lot to enhance the design of the ball. For instance, border-print fabrics can add a unique touch. The motifs on the border prints shown here have been carefully centered inside the template shape so that the fabric acts as a frame around the highlighted shape. *World Without End* and *Job's Troubles* each use this technique. In *World Without End*, the Template 2 square is divided down into four triangles. Each triangle is then centered on a mirror-imaged motif in the border print. Finally, the four identical triangles are put together to reform the square, creating a lovely new design. In *Job's Trouble*, the Template 5 octagon is broken down into eight smaller triangles. Each triangle in any one octagon is cut from an identical mirror imaged portion of the border print, then the eight triangles are sewn together to reform the original shape.

To try this technique, begin by drawing the original template shape for the ball (square, octagon, etc.) without seam allowances. Divide the shape into triangles, as explained above. Then, make a new template for the resulting triangle, drawing a guideline through the center. Add ¼" seam allowance around all sides. Position the template on the fabric so that the guideline centers on the desired motif. Trace part of the motif onto the template—this will help you find the exact same motif when you cut the remaining fabric pieces. Cut all the triangles you need from fabric, making sure they are identical. Sew the triangles together, carefully matching motifs in the fabric, to create the original fabric shape.

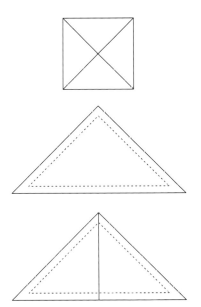

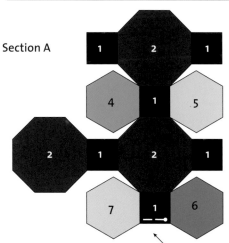

Section A

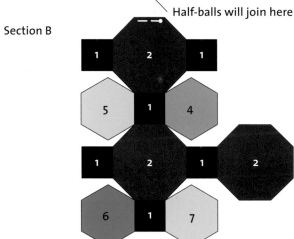

Section B

Half-balls will join here

from Fabrics 3 to 6) using **Template 4.** Templates include ¼" seam allowance. Speed up cutting time by using the pre-made template set that accompanies this book.

Solving the Puzzle

The easiest way to construct this ball is to sew two halves and then stitch the two halves together. Follow these steps:

1. Lay out the fabrics for Section A and Section B, taking care to follow the color placement in the diagram. Note that Section B is an exact mirror image of Section A. Mark or place pins in the bottom-most Fabric 1 square in Section A and in the top-most

Fabric 2 octagon in Section B. Once both halves of the ball are complete, this is where you begin sewing them together.

2. Stitch the pieces in rows as shown, then join the rows. Press lightly.

3. Sew the sides of the hexagons to the sides of the octagons and squares as shown, creating a half-ball shape.

4. Right sides together, orient the two halves so that pre-marked Fabrics 1 and 2 are aligned. Pin the seam. Carefully sew the halves together, pivoting pieces where necessary. Sew until only one pentagon side remains unstitched.

5. Carefully turn the ball right side out. Stuff and finish (see pages 12–15).

Step 3

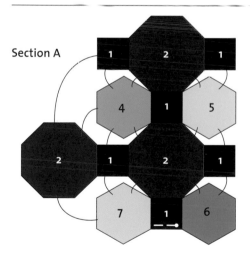

Section A

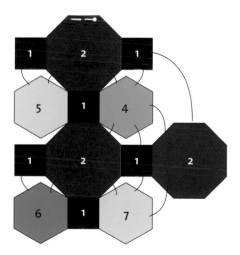

Section B

Block Patchwork

Mathematical model: *Rhombicosidodecahedron*

Diameter: 7"   **Templates 1, 2, and 3**

*This ball is almost identical in design to a pattern named **Block Patchwork**, originally published in the 1898 Ladies' Art Company Catalog. The only difference is that the hexagon changes to a pentagon in order to get a spherical shape. Just as in **Job's Trouble** on page 46, this design requires three templates.*

Color Clues

There are several different possibilities for coloring *Block Patchwork*. One option is to limit the ball to just three colors—the triangles are made from one fabric, the squares from another, and the pentagons from a third fabric. If you wish you can use as many as eight different fabrics. The triangles are all from the same dark fabric. The squares are from a slightly lighter fabric. The pentagons are made from six bright and light fabrics. Like most of the designs in *Patchwork Puzzle Balls*, the finished ball has same-color pentagons lying directly opposite each other. Unlike other designs, the same-color pentagons do not touch each other, so there can be less contrast than usual in the fabrics selected for Fabrics 3 to 8. Copy the fabric chart on page 88 and staple or glue your fabric swatches to it.

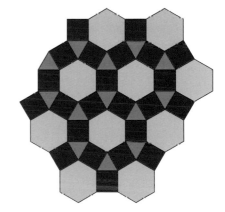

Traditional pattern

Cutting Clues

Cut **30 squares** from Fabric 1 using **Template 2** on page 85. Cut **20 triangles** from Fabric 2 using **Template 1**. Cut **12 pentagons** (2 each from Fabrics 3 to 8) using **Template 3.** Templates include ¼" seam allowance. Speed up cutting time by using the pre-made template set that accompanies this book.

Solving the Puzzle

The easiest way to construct this ball is to sew two halves and then stitch the two halves together. Follow these steps:

1. Lay out the fabric shapes for Section A and Section B as shown. Carefully follow the number sequence in the diagram to ensure proper color placement.

Step 2

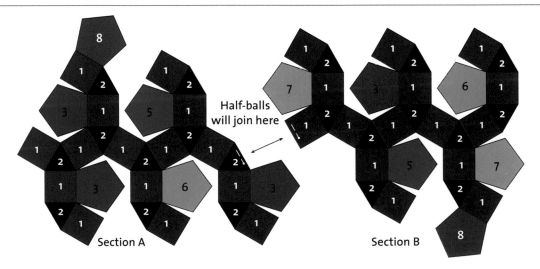

Half-balls will join here

Section A

Section B

2. Mark or place pins in the top right-most Fabric 2 in Section A and in the bottom left-most Fabric 1 in Section B. Once both halves of the ball are complete, this is where you will begin sewing them together.
3. Sew all the pieces in each half together as shown. Press.
4. Join the sides of the shapes together as shown, creating a half-ball shape.
5. Right sides together, orient the halves to that pre-marked Fabrics 2 and 1 are aligned. Pin the seam. Carefully sew the halves together, pivoting the fabric as necessary. Sew until only one pentagon side remains unstitched.
6. Carefully turn the ball right side out. Stuff and finish (see pages 12–15).

SMILE, YOU'RE ON CAMERA!

Photographs are always a great gift. Why not incorporate your favorite pictures into a ball? Many manufacturers offer paper-backed fabric that can go right through a color printer or copy machine. (Check individual products for instructions on use.) When the photo is in place, simply peel off the paper and cut the fabric as you would any other. This is a wonderful way to capture memories of a special event. Imagine putting your vacation snap shots onto a ball for your child to play with when the holiday is over. Or, for a loved one in a nursing home, a soft ball pillow with photos of family members makes a cherished gift. Carole Nicholas made this version of *Job's Trouble*.

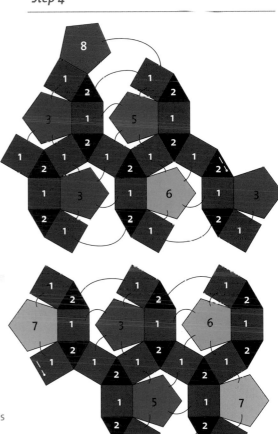

Step 4

Beyond the Basics

THE BALLS IN THE FIRST SECTION of this book use simple shapes, like a triangle, square, pentagon, hexagon and octagon. Now that you are comfortable with the basic techniques, you are ready to work with slightly more complex shapes. The four designs that follow may appear more challenging, but remember that they are constructed in exactly the same way. The first two patterns, *Tumbling Blocks* and *Desert Rose* are still quite simple. The last two—*Whirligig* and *ZZZs*—require fairly advanced piecing skills and are best done by hand.

Tumbling Blocks

Mathematical model: *Rhombic triacontahedron*   **Diameter:** 5"

Template 6

***Tumbling Blocks** is one of my all-time favorite quilting patterns. The design is made up of 60° diamonds and is pieced with three distinctly different values or colors, which are always oriented in identical positions. When you look at the ball, it seems to be made of the same 60°/120° diamond used in the popular quilt pattern. However, that precise angle results in a patchwork design that is completely flat, not spherical. After much experimentation, I discovered that the correct shape to use to create a patchwork ball shape has angles of 64.26°/116.34°. The template on page 86 is exactly that size.*

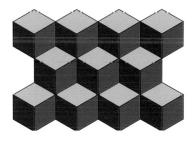

Traditional pattern

Color Clues

Five distinctly different fabrics must be used for this ball. Each fabric touches every one of the others, so if they are too close in color or value, the design will not show up. Pay special attention to the layout diagram to make sure that no two pieces of the same fabric are positioned next to each other. The design of the ball has the same color diamonds lying directly opposite each other. Copy the Fabric Chart on page 88 and staple or glue swatches of your fabric selections to it.

Cutting Clues

Cut **30 diamonds** (six from each of five fabrics) using **Template 6** on page 86. Template includes ¼" seam allowance.

Solving the Puzzle

The easiest way to construct this ball is to sew two halves, then stitch them together. Follow these steps:

1. Lay out five units made up of three diamonds each, carefully following the color placement shown on diagrams for Sections A and B. Maintain this order of placement to ensure that same-color fabrics do not touch each other. Stitch each three-diamond unit together.

2. Connect three-diamond units for each section as shown. Mark or place pins in the bottom-most Fabric 1 in Section A, and in the

Step 1

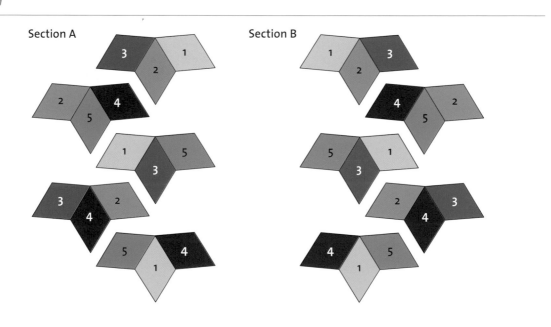

top-most Fabric 3 in Section B. Once both halves of the ball are complete, this is where you will begin sewing them together.

3. Following the lines in the diagram, sew the remaining seams, creating a half-ball shape.

4. Right sides together, orient the halves so that pre-marked Fabrics 1 and 3 are aligned. Pin the seam. Carefully sew the halves together, pivoting the fabric at each side of the diamonds. Sew until only one seam remains unstitched.

5. Carefully turn the ball right side out. Stuff and finish (see pages 12–15).

Step 2

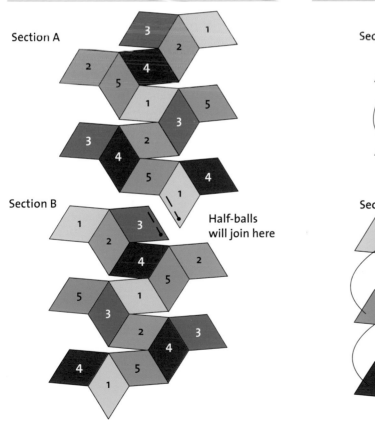

Section A

Section B

Half-balls will join here

Step 3

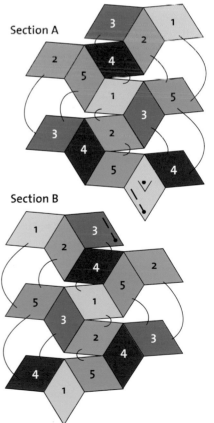

Section A

Section B

61

Desert Rose

Mathematical model: *Pentagonal icosatetrahedron*

Diameter: 7"   **Template 7**

Desert Rose *is a popular quilt pattern based on a variation of a hexagon. Our spherical version shown here, made by Barbara Hollinger, uses what appears to be the exact same shape. However, you will notice that the quilt pattern has six petals to the flower and the ball pattern has only five. The angles of the shape used for the quilt pattern are 60° and 120°, whereas the angles needed to form the ball are 67.328° and 118.8°. The pattern for the ball is made up of twelve five-petal flowers, with all petals in each flower made from the same fabric. There are two flowers in each of six fabrics, and same-color flowers lie opposite each other on the ball.*

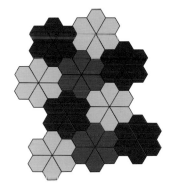

Traditional pattern

Color Clues

Six distinctly different fabrics must be used for *Desert Rose*. Each fabric touches every one of the others, so if they are too close in color or value, the flowers will not stand out. Copy the Fabric Chart on page 88 and staple or glue small pieces of your fabric selections to it.

Cutting Clues

Cut **60 patches** (ten from each of six fabrics) using **Template 7** on page 87. Template includes ¼" seam allowance.

Solving the Puzzle

You will begin by making the ten individual flower shapes that make up the ball. This will help ensure that the points meet nicely at the center of each flower. Next, the flowers are sewn into two distinct halves of the ball, which are then sewn together. Follow these steps:

1. Sew five same-color petals together to form each flower. Make a total of twelve flowers, two in each color. Note that the flowers will not lie flat; they will be slightly cupped.

2. Lay out the flowers as shown for each ball half (Section A and Section B). Carefully follow the color placement in the diagram to make sure that same-color flowers lie opposite each other on the ball and do not touch each other. Mark or place pins in the bottom-most petal of Flower 6 in Section A and in the top-right petal of Flower 3 in Section B. Once both halves of the ball are complete, this is where you will begin sewing them together.

3. For each section, sew the shapes together following the lines in the diagram, creating a half-ball shape.

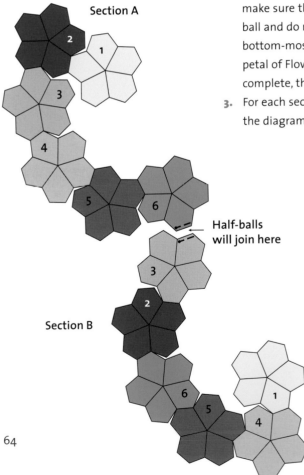

Section A

Half-balls
will join here

Section B

64

4. Right sides together, orient the halves so that pre-marked petals of Flowers 6 and 3 are aligned. Pin the seam. Sew the halves together until only one seam remains unstitched.

5. Carefully turn the ball right side out. Stuff and finish (see pages 12–15).

Step 3

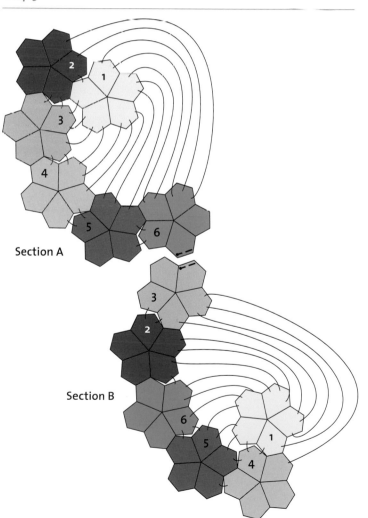

Section A

Section B

ADDING APPLIQUE!

Terri Willet used decorative appliqué to embellish her version of *Desert Rose*. Before sewing the pieces of the ball together, she appliquéd motifs cut from a paisley fabric onto each of the pieces, using a technique known as *soft-edge piecing*.

Whirligig

Mathematical model: *Icosahedron* family   **Diameter:** 7″

Templates 1 and 8

This tessellating design—a pattern in which all pieces interlock perfectly—is similar to the traditional quilt pattern, also known as **Whirligig**. *The difference is that the shape used for the quilt pattern has six "arms", while this one has only three.* **Whirligig** *is different from all of the other designs in* **Patchwork Puzzle Balls** *in that four pieces make up the basic shape. When you have cut out the pieces, it really is a puzzle to figure out how they will join together!*

Traditional pattern

Color Clues

Five different fabrics are required for *Whirligig*. If you study the photograph, you will see that each Y shape touches all the others. This means it is important to carefully select fabrics so that all the pieces will be easily distinguishable. Also note that the placement of the colors is evenly distributed around the ball, so be sure to follow the diagrams when sewing. Copy the fabric chart on page 88 and glue or staple swatches of the five fabrics to it.

Cutting Clues

Cut **20 triangles** (four from each of five fabrics) using **Template 1** and **60 pieces** (twelve from each of five fabrics) using **Template 8** on page 87. Make sure that all pieces cut are identical (not reversed). Template includes ¼″ seam allowance.

Solving the Puzzle

The ball is constructed in two halves. Once the two halves are complete, you may think that you made a mistake, because there will be definite "points" sticking out and you may wonder if the ball will end up round. Don't worry—when the ball is well stuffed, it will transform into a perfect sphere. Follow theses steps:

1. Stitch four whirligigs in each color as shown.
2. Organize the whirligigs for Sections A and B into rows as shown.
3. Sew the rows together to complete each section. Mark or place pins in the right-most Fabric 4 in Section A and in the left-most

Step 1

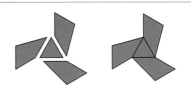

Step 2

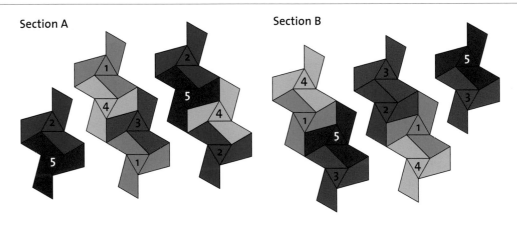

68

Fabric 1 in Section B. Once both halves of the ball are complete, this is where you will begin sewing them together. Press lightly.

4. Connect the whirligigs as indicated by the lines in the diagram, creating a half-ball shape.

5. Right sides together, orient the two halves so that pre-marked Fabrics 4 and 1 are aligned. Pin the seam. Sew the halves together, pivoting the fabric as needed. Sew until only one seam remains unstitched.

6. Carefully turn the ball right side out. Stuff and finish (see pages 12–15).

Step 2

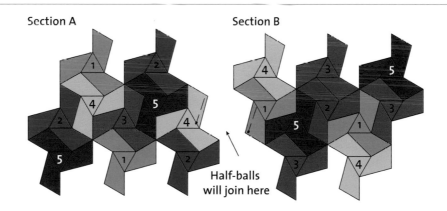

Section A   Section B

Half-balls will join here

Step 3

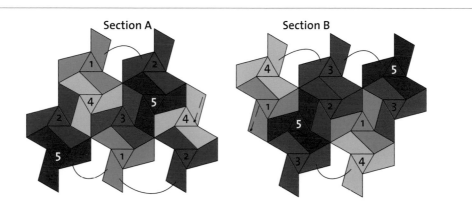

Section A   Section B

ZZZs

Mathematical model: *Rhombic triacontahedron* family   **Diameter:** 7″
Templates 9 and 10

There are a variety of patchwork patterns that piece together fabrics to form letters. **ZZZs** *now takes that idea one step further and turns the repeating letter Z into interlocking pieces that form the ball. The design was created by transforming the 64.26°/116.34° diamond that made up the* **Tumbling Blocks** *ball.*

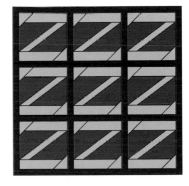

Traditional pattern

Color Clues

Five distinct fabrics must be used for ZZZs. Each fabric touches every one of the others, so if your selections are too close in color or value, the design will not show up. Pay special attention to the layout diagram to avoid this. The design of the ball has the same color Zs lying directly opposite each other. Copy the Fabric Chart on page 88 and staple or glue the fabric swatches to it.

Cutting Clues

Cut **30 patches** (six from each of five fabrics) using **Template 9** and **60 patches** (twelve from each of five fabrics) using **Template 10** on page 87. Make sure that all pieces cut are identical (not reversed). Make sure to add seam allowances on all sides, as indicated on templates.

Solving the Puzzle

The easiest way to construct this ball is to first make the individual Zs, then sew the Zs together in groups of three. Sew these units together to create half-ball shapes, then stitch the halves together. Follow these steps:

1. Make six same-color Zs by stitching two Template 10 pieces to Template 9 piece as shown. Repeat for each of five colors.

2. Organize the Zs for Sections A and B by laying out five three-Z units for each section. Stitch each unit.

3. Connect five three-Z units for Sections A and B as shown. Mark or place pins in the bottom-most Fabric 1 in Section A and in the top-right Fabric 3 in Section B. Once both halves of the ball are complete, this is where you will begin sewing them together. Press lightly.

4. Connect the Z units as indicated by the lines in the diagram, creating a half-ball shape.

Step 1

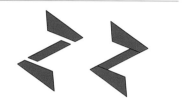

Step 2

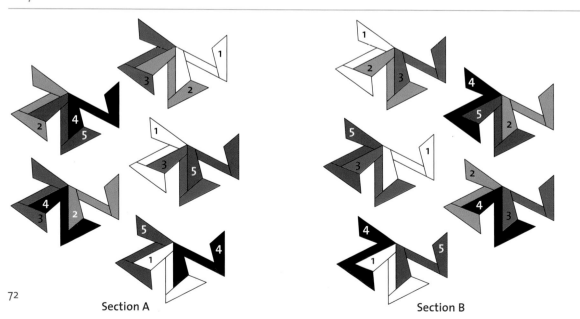

Section A

Section B

5. Right sides together, orient the two halves so that pre-marked Fabrics 1 and 3 are aligned. Pin the seam. Sew the halves together, pivoting the fabric at each side of each angle on the Zs. Sew until only one seam remains unstitched.

6. Carefully turn the ball right side out. Stuff and finish (see pages 12–15).

Step 3

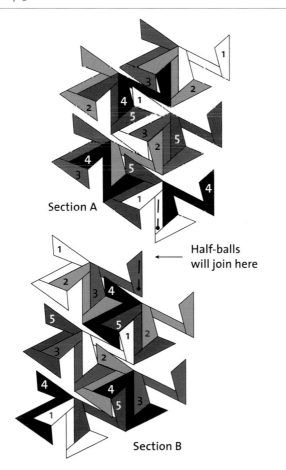

Section A

Section B

Half-balls will join here

Step 4

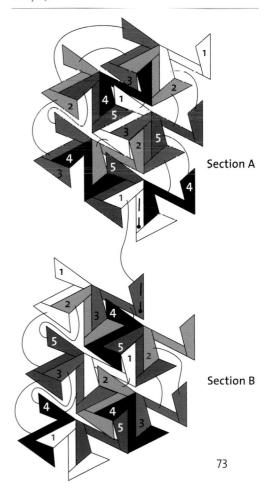

Section A

Section B

Drafting Multi-Sized Balls

THE TEMPLATES PROVIDED in *Patchwork Puzzle Balls* allow for each design to be made up only in the size specified in the pattern. At times, you may want to make a particular ball in a new size. With some basic drafting skills, resizing the patterns is easy to do. If you have a graphics program that draws polygons, simply specify a shape with three, four, five, six , or eight sides, in whatever size you desire. The only rule to remember is if there are multiple shapes in the design, the lengths of the sides of each one must be the same.

While reading about *polyhedra*, I came across a rather intriguing way to draft all five basic shapes in *Patchwork Puzzle Balls* using just a pencil, paper, ruler, right angle rule, and compass. When I figured out how to do this, I was amazed at the puzzle of the universe in which these magical shapes are so intertwined. Even if you do not intend to draft designs by hand, I think you will find the relationship of basic shapes to one another and the ease of drafting them fascinating.

Step-by-Step Drafting

To draft any basic shape in *Patchwork Puzzle Balls* to a new size, follow the steps below. Remember that for different-shaped patches to sew together perfectly, their sides must share a common length. Before you begin, decide what length you would like the sides to be.

Draft Triangle

1. Setting your compass to the desired length, draw a circle. The radius of the circle will be exact length of the side of the shape you are drafting. Mark the center (A).

2. Draw a line straight through the middle of the circle.

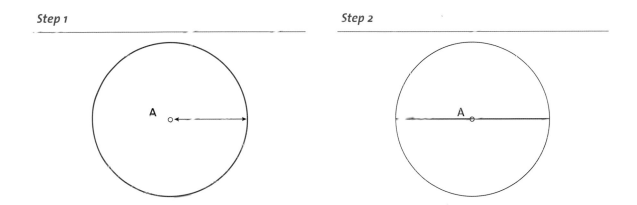

Step 1

Step 2

Draft Triangle (continued)

3. With the radius setting on the compass unchanged, place the point on the edge of the circle where the line touches it (Point B). Draw a second circle exactly the same size as the first, intersecting A as shown. Mark C at the top intersection and D at the bottom intersection.

4. Draw a line from A to C and from B to C to get a perfect equilateral triangle, with all sides of the previously specified length.

Step 3

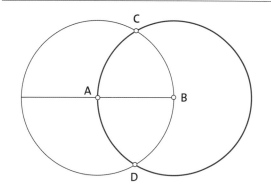

Step 4

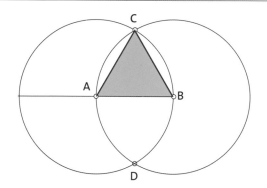

Draft Square

5. Place a right-angle rule on line AB, with the angle at A. Draw a line straight up until it hits the top of the circle.

6. Flip the rule so that the right angle is now at B. Again, draw a line straight up until it hits the top of the circle.

7. Draw a line to connect the two new points and complete a perfect square.

Step 5

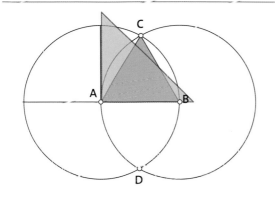

Step 6

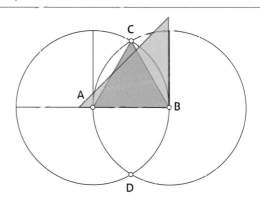

Step 7

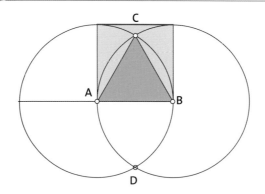

Draft Hexagon

8. Draw a vertical line from D to C, extending it beyond C. Divide the square diagonally from corner to corner as indicated by the dotted lines. Extend the dotted lines outwards beyond the square. Mark the center of the square (E).

9. Draw lines along the sides of the triangle, extending them beyond the triangle as shown.

10. Place the point of the compass at E (center of square). Open it out to A or B and draw a smaller circle that touches A and B and the upper corners of the square. Mark the point where the circle touches line CD as point F.

11. Place the point of the compass at C (top of triangle) and open it out to A or B. Draw a larger circle (same size as Step 3 circles). Mark points G, H, I, and J.

12. Connect A, G, H, I, J, and B to draw a perfect hexagon with sides of the previously specified length.

Step 8

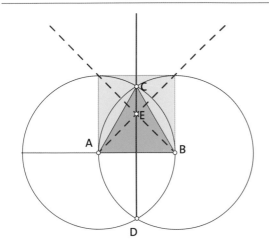

Step 9

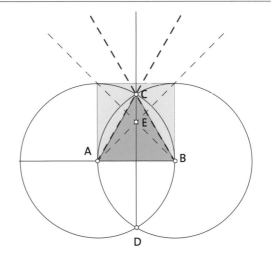

Step 10

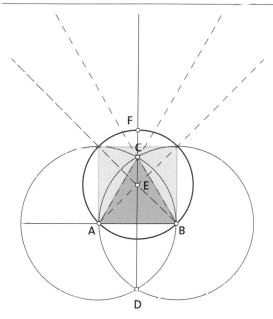

Step 11

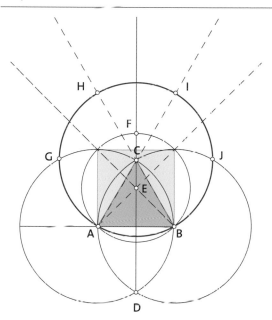

Step 12

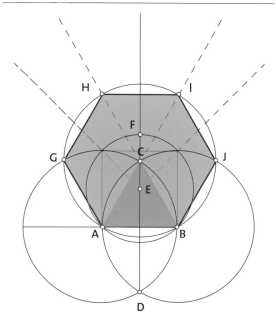

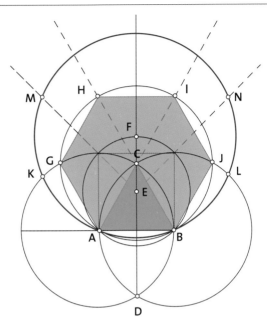

Draft Octagon

13. Place the point of the compass at F and open it out to either A or B. Draw a still larger circle. Mark M and N where the circle intersects with the dotted lines extending from the diagonals of the square. Mark K and L where the new circle intersects the two original circles.

14. Extend the sides of the square until the lines intersect the new circle at O and P.

15. Connect A, K, M, O, P, N, L, and B to draw a perfect octagon.

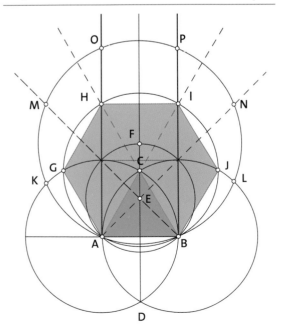

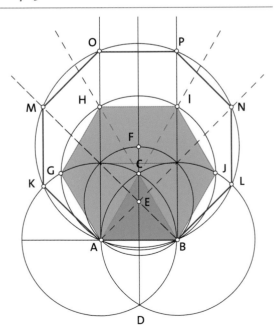

Draft Pentagon

16. Draw a line from K to L. Mark the point where the line touches the center vertical line as point Q.

17. Place the point of the compass on Q. Open it out to A or B and draw a circle. Mark with dots all five points where the new circle touches the vertical line and the two original circles.

18. Connect the dots to draw a perfect pentagon.

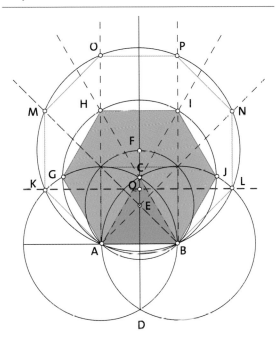

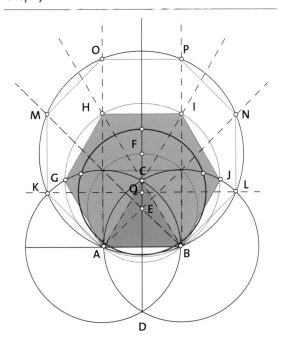

Step 17

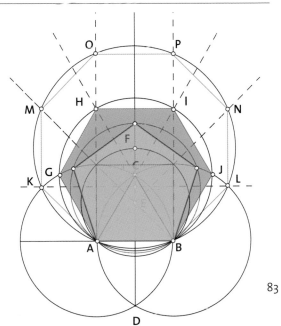

Step 18

83

Making New Templates

Once you have created new shapes with a common side length, make a new set of templates by simple adding ¼" seam allowance around all sides of each shape. Follow the directions on page 7–8 to make new templates.

Templates

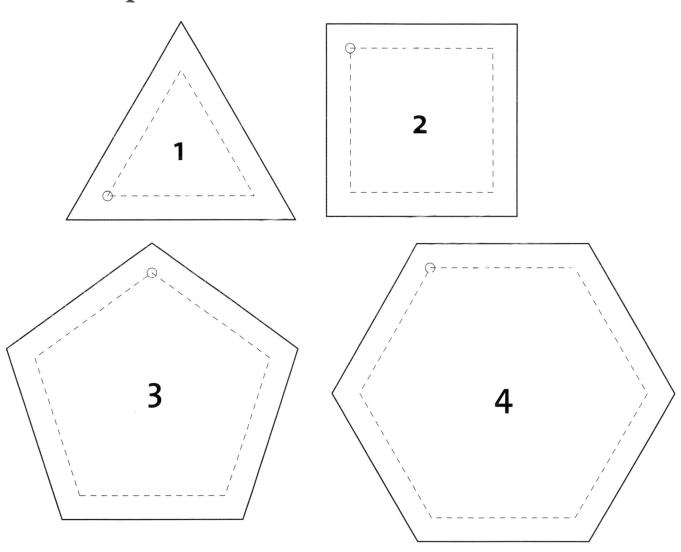

Templates

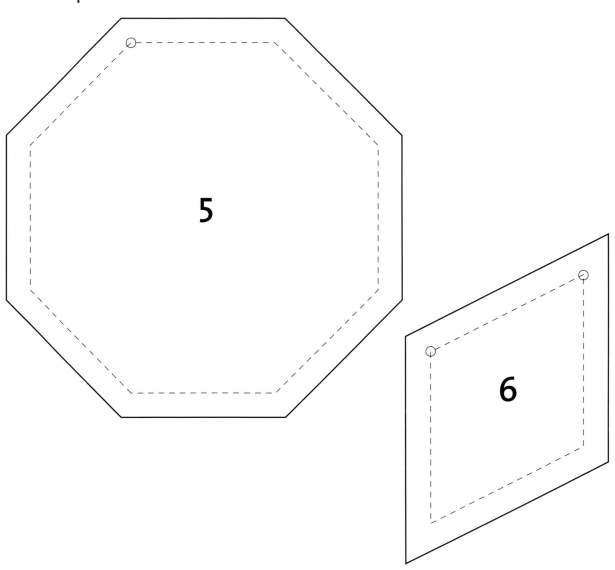

5

6

Templates

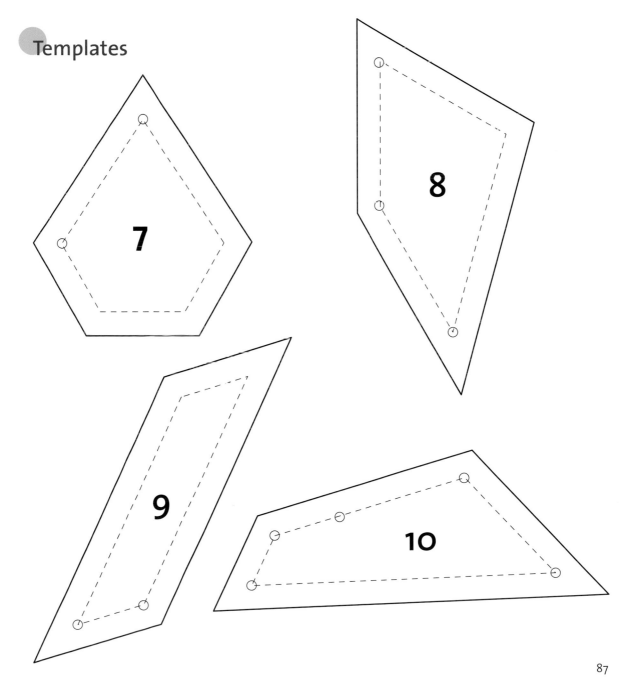

Fabric Chart

Fabric 1

Fabric 2

Fabric 3

Fabric 4

Fabric 5

Fabric 6

Fabric 7

Fabric 8

Bibliography

W.W. Rouse Ball and H.S.M Coxeter, *Mathematical Recreations and Essays*, General Publishing Company, Ltd., Toronto, Ontario, Canada, 1974

Jinny Beyer, *Designing Tessellations*, Contemporary Books, Chicago, 1999

Jinny Beyer, *Quiltmaking by Hand*, Breckling Press, Elmhurst (Chicago), 2004

H.S.M. Coxeter, P. Du Val, H.T. Flather, and J.F. Petrie, *The Fifty-Nine Icosahedra*, Tarquin Publications, Norfolk, England, 1938

Keith Critchlow, *Order in Space*, Thames and Hudson Inc., New York, 1969

Peter R. Cromwell, *Polyhedra*, Cambridge University Press, 1997

H.M. Cundy, A.P. Rollett, *Mathematical Models*, Tarquin Publications, Norfolk, England, 1951

Alan Holden, *Shapes, Space, and Symmetry*, Columbia University Press, 1971